KINGDOM EXPLOSION

I0517697

THE PRESENCE, POWER, AND POSSIBILITIES

OF THE KINGDOM OF GOD

PETER JOHN BROOKS

KINGDOM EXPLOSION: The Presence, Power, and Possibilities of the Kingdom of God

Scripture taken from the New King James Version® unless otherwise noted. Copyright © 1982 by Thomas Nelson. Used by permission. All rights reserved.

Print ISBN: 978-1-968804-05-3

Digital ISBN: 978-1-968804-04-6

Published by Fivestone New Media

www.bethelcornerstone.org

Contents

Introduction

JESUS CAME to remake the world. He came to stop Satan from ruining his Father's creation, end the reign of sin, rescue humanity from evil, and make everything new. The divine power for world transformation that Jesus unleashed is called the kingdom of God.

Jesus taught more about the kingdom of God than any other subject. He wanted people to understand God's kingdom so they could experience its power. Jesus is a practical teacher, and he not only taught about the kingdom but he demonstrated it. He saved the lost, healed the sick, cast out demons, and raised the dead. Through teaching and action, Jesus proved that the kingdom of God can completely transform the world.

Nothing could block Jesus from accomplishing his purpose. When he went to the cross, Satan threw all the forces of darkness at him, but not even death could hold Christ down. Even though all sin and evil covered him, he rose up from the grave, crushing the power of hell and displaying the irresistible power of God over everything. Resurrection proved that Jesus is the king of kings and gave unassailable testimony that God's kingdom is going to dominate the entire earth.

"Seek first the kingdom of God," Jesus said (Matthew 6:33).

Jesus wants us to continue the kingdom work that he began. The kingdom of God is supposed to be the main priority of our lives, taking precedence above everything else— money, family, happiness, or security. Christ wants us to subordinate our entire lives to the pursuit of the kingdom of God.

The kingdom of God is *the place where God is king*. God's kingdom is the place where his rule is revealed and his authority prevails. In the kingdom of God, God reigns. Wherever God is king, there is his kingdom.

Seeking the kingdom of God means seeking for this God to dominate the world and transform it. It means looking for God's rule to come into the places that it's not, swallow up things contrary to him, and leave righteousness and peace in its wake.

"Thy kingdom come" (Matthew 6:10).

Jesus wants us to pray for the kingdom of God to come. We are to pray for current conditions on the earth to be radically altered by the power of the gospel. We are to pray for God's reign to expand on the earth and Satan's rule to be broken: "God, dominate this broken world and heal it, and let your kingdom come everywhere." Like any other prayer, we are to pray this prayer in faith, expecting that it will actually happen.

As Christians, we're not just trying to make it through life and get to heaven. If we're born again, we are already inside the kingdom of God (Colossians 1:13). God's kingdom is not just something for the future; it's a reality now, and Jesus wants us to dedicate our lives to its manifestation.

God is looking for radical, fiery saints who will "seize the kingdom of God" (Matthew 11:12). We're called to seize spiritual land from the devil and plant the flag of God's kingdom into new territory on this earth. God wants us to spread his word on the earth and do his works. This is possible because the Holy Spirit is inside us.

"Most assuredly, I say to you, he who believes in Me, the works that I do he will do also; and greater works than these he will do, because I go to My Father" (John 14:12).

Heal the sick, cast out demons, and raise the dead. God can do these things and more through his people. As Christians do greater works than Jesus, the kingdom of God will mount a final assault against all fortresses of Satan in this world. There is to be no limit to our pursuit of the kingdom of God, because ultimately the kingdom of God will take over everything.

The current age will culminate with Christ's return to the earth and the revelation of God's kingdom all over the world. Until that glorious day when Christ reigns over everything, the kingdom of God is in the earth, but not in fullness. It's here in measure, but not completely. Now, God wants his kingdom to advance or 'come' into the places it's not. He wants it to grow and expand in the earth. This tremendous objective, which defined the ministry of Jesus, is to govern our lives. We must keep praying, keep seeking, and keep believing for the kingdom of God to come all over the world until it actually does.

Whenever the kingdom of God comes into a place, Jesus is exalted, and his redemption is revealed. People are restored to God, and the powers of spiritual darkness are broken. God wants to reign over everything. He wants his kingdom to be everywhere, and for everyone and everything to bow down to the awesome name of Jesus. Let's work together with the Holy Spirit in fulfilling this awesome purpose. It's the main reason we're here on this earth.

I.

A Brief History of the Kingdom of God

IN THE BEGINNING, the kingdom of God dominated the world. Glory covered the earth, and the kingdom of God was everywhere. Adam and Eve completely submitted to God, and they had indomitable spiritual power. Their words were powerful, charged with divine force. Their actions were weighty, replete with supernatural results. Through the might of the Holy Spirit, they ruled the world, managing the creation and maintaining its glorious order (Genesis 1:28).

Divine power establishes God's kingdom upon the earth. "The kingdom of God is not in word, but in power" (1 Corinthians 4:20).

Satan hated humanity and despised their spiritual power. He wanted to cut Adam and Eve off from God, eradicate God's kingdom from the earth, and take over the world.

Satan slithered up to Eve like a snake. He whispered, "You don't need to submit to God constantly. This whole submission-to-God thing is holding you back. If you have the guts to do what you want, you will become like God!"

Eve was mesmerized. Up to that point, she and Adam had always been looking to God and doing whatever he wanted. Submission was the source of their spiritual power. But the wily serpent made the woman wonder if there was a better way.

Eve came near the tree of the knowledge of good and evil. God said this tree was deadly, but like everything else he had made, he also said it was "very good" (Genesis 1:31). It was good because it guaranteed that humanity had free will. If Adam and Eve wanted to, they could eat from the tree of the knowledge of good and evil and leave the garden. The consequences would be disastrous, but God wasn't going to stop them. Paradise was not a prison. It was a place of free will and genuine love, which meant escape was possible.

Satan's suggestion lodged in Eve's mind. She thought about the tree of knowledge of good and evil, desired to taste its luscious fruit, and dreamed about becoming like God. She thought she was missing out on something big. She went up to the tree, plucked the forbidden fruit, and ate it. She convinced Adam to eat it too.

The moment the fruit entered their bodies, Adam and Eve died. "The wages of sin is death" (Romans 6:23). Spiritual death was sudden, as Adam and Eve were cut off from God. Divine presence and power drained out of their lives. They became spiritually impotent. Their words became hollow, and their actions became weak. They were empty shells of their former vibrant selves. They were no longer backed up by the power of God or the armies of heaven. Without divine power, they were no longer able to represent God's kingdom to the world.

With humanity spiritually defeated, the kingdom of God vanished from the earth like a puff of smoke.

The Kingdom of Darkness

Satan became the new prince of the world (John 12:31). Fallen angels swarmed over the earth, establishing their dark empire. The curse devoured everything alive. Animals began to attack each other. Roses sprouted thorns. Mosquitoes developed a taste for blood. Bees got their stings. Thistles took the place of beautiful, tender flowers. Disease, decay, and death corrupted the world. God's exquisite creation began to groan in pain (Romans 8:22) under the dominion of darkness. The creation became a slave of futility (Romans 8:20) and could no longer glorify God.

Adam and Eve had children and grandchildren, and pain spread throughout their generations. As people multiplied on the earth, they cried under the reign of darkness. Famine shattered communities. War destroyed nations. Disease wiped out entire civilizations. Death cut off the life of every man and woman.

The torments of sin weren't just Adam's fault; they were everyone's fault. Every time someone sinned (and everyone did), the gates of hell were opened afresh, and more and more evil flooded into the world. The gangrene of sin brought multiplying problems which kept trooping into the world without intermission. People were often blind to the cause of these problems; they didn't know sin was the root cause. Even if they did, they kept on sinning and couldn't stop themselves even if they tried. Sin not only brought death into the world but caused every evil thing that leads up to death. Its disastrous repercussions affected everyone everywhere.

Humanity desperately tried to find solutions. They refused God but tried to appease Satan, their dark Lord. They developed religious rituals like those found in the Vedas and constructed megalithic religious centers like Stonehenge. They offered human sacrifices— from America to Europe to China— hoping to ward off evil and obtain help from the 'gods.'

Satan just laughed at their foolishness and tormented them even more.

Humanity tried other ways to solve their problems. They developed technologies in metallurgy, agriculture, and medicine. They tried to grow more food, stay warmer and safer, and make their toil lighter. Technology helped, but it couldn't resolve their main challenges. People still got sick, fought with each other, and were plagued by evil. As long as they refused God's reign, they suffered. As long as they sinned, they died.

God encouraged people to return to him and be healed. He inspired great preachers in every generation. Enoch proclaimed truth. Noah preached righteousness. But people didn't want to listen.

God's kingdom was unable to get a foothold in the earth. Soon unimaginable evil took over, and God had no choice but wipe it all away and start again. He sent the Great Flood and destroyed everything except what was in Noah's boat.

The Flood brought judgment, but not redemption. The waters cleansed the earth, but not the human heart. After the water dried up, people multiplied and spread over the world again; but sin and its accompanying torments multiplied just as fast as humanity reproduced. Satan continued his brutal reign.

God kept reaching out. Over the centuries he sent prophets to many nations, especially to Israel, urging them to forsake sin and serve God alone. "God loves you. If you obey God, you will see his kingdom and blessing come back to the world!" But people refused to repent. They killed God's prophets, rejected his word, and continued embracing Satan, their murderer. They flagellated themselves with the results of their evil choices, and then they gave the whip to Satan so he could beat them even more. They spat on God's face, hating the one who loved them and tried to help them.

The Seed of the Woman

Only God could remove the thick cloak of sin. Long ago, right after the Fall, God promised that a Redeemer would come and crush the head of Satan.

> And I will put enmity between you [Satan] and the woman, and between your seed and her Seed [Christ]; He shall bruise your head, and you shall bruise His heel. (Genesis 3:15)

Many cultures remembered this primeval prophecy and enshrined their memories in twisted mythological stories about a great conqueror who would destroy the terrible snake. These stories are imperfectly remembered throughout the world and are found in various forms in many cultures.

The Bible is the only perfect record of this ancient promise, and it records that the Seed of the woman would someday crush Satan's head.

Two thousand years ago, it was time for the Seed of God - *Messiah* in the Hebrew and *Christ* in Greek - to come. The eternal Son of God who created the world laid aside his glory in heaven as if putting off a dazzling robe and came to earth as a baby in a womb.

Jesus was conceived by a virgin, signifying that he would redeem the world by the power of God, not by the power of man. His birthplace was Bethlehem, a town whose name means "fruitful house of bread." He was born in an animal feeding trough, symbolizing that he was the bread of God that would feed the world. His name is "Jesus" which means "God saves."

Jesus was a glorious king, but most people didn't know it. He wore ordinary clothes, befriended common people, and stayed in humble homes. He didn't possess the accoutrements of royalty like armies and gold, for the tools of human power were irrelevant to his reign.

Humble Beginnings

When Jesus was about 30 years old, he was baptized at the Jordan River and filled with the Holy Spirit. He was now going to walk on the earth as the Christ, the Son of God, the Savior of the world. His words became charged with the force of heaven. His actions carried the weight of God. He was a man armed with the power of the Almighty, living and moving upon the earth. He had recovered the ancient power that was able to manifest the kingdom of God upon the earth - the power that Adam had lost. Not a man since Adam had this spiritual power, and Christ was about to shock the world.

God-manifest-in-flesh returned to his hometown Nazareth, where everyone knew him as a carpenter. He entered the weekly synagogue meeting and stood up. His friends, relatives, and neighbors gaped at him. He began reading from Isaiah the prophet:

> The Spirit of the Lord is upon me, because he has anointed me to preach the gospel to the poor; he hath sent me to heal the brokenhearted, to preach deliverance to the captives, and recovering of sight to the blind, to set at liberty them that are bruised, to preach the acceptable year of the Lord. (Luke 4:18-19)

Jesus explained that this Scripture referred to him. He was the one God had sent to rescue the world. He was anointed with the Holy Spirit. He was the Seed of the woman - the Messiah!

His family, friends, and neighbors were shocked.

"How can this man whom we have known since childhood claim to be the Messiah?"

They became indignant.

They violently attacked him. They didn't care if this was a religious meeting. It was time to kill! They yanked Jesus out onto the road, dragged him out of town, and brought him to the edge of a cliff. They were about to throw the Messiah, whom they had been eagerly praying and waiting for, down to his death.

> So all those in the synagogue, when they heard these things, were filled with wrath, and rose up and thrust Him out of the city; and they led Him to the brow of the hill on which their city was built, that they might throw Him down over the cliff. (Luke 4:28-29)

These Nazarenes had no idea that they were trying to murder God. They were blind, enslaved by the devil. They were repeating the cycle of lunacy and self-torture that each generation of humanity had perpetuated since the Fall, rejecting life and light, and choosing darkness and death.

At the edge of the cliff, Jesus was about to be killed, just like God's prophets had been murdered throughout history. It seemed as though the Messiah's ministry would be stopped before it ever got started.

But Jesus was armed with supreme spiritual power, and this made him unstoppable. He immobilized the crazy crowd. Suddenly, they couldn't hold onto him or grab his clothes. Maybe he became invisible. He walked right through the midst of them, leaving them and their mad frenzy behind.

"Then passing through the midst of them, He went His way" (Luke 4:30).

From the edge of a cliff where he was about to be killed, Jesus began his public ministry. With no power but the Holy Spirit, he proceeded to go throughout Israel, revealing the love, mercy, and power of God. Humanity often hated him, but he was going to redeem them anyway, and there was nothing they could do to stop him.

Through Jesus, the kingdom of God had begun its inexorable march toward total world domination.

What Adam lost, Jesus would win back. Eden was going to be restored to the earth.

- Kingdom Core -

1. The kingdom of God is the place where God is king.

2. The kingdom of God once dominated the earth when Adam and Eve walked in divine spiritual power.

3. When Adam and Eve sinned, they lost spiritual power, and the kingdom of God disappeared from the earth.

4. Jesus Christ was anointed with spiritual power to rescue the creation from the dominion of darkness and restore the kingdom of God to the earth.

- Prayer -

Heavenly Father, praise you for your wisdom and power. You created this world out of nothing, and you can do anything even now. Sin brought death, but you bring life. You are stronger than all evil. Your kingdom is going to dominate this world, and nothing can stop it. Thank you for sending your Son Jesus to rescue me and deliver this world from sin. He is the only hope for this world. Jesus is the answer for every problem this world faces, and nothing else is going to work. Open my eyes to see the infinite power that operates through Jesus. Help me understand how this divine spiritual power will expand your kingdom on earth. Your kingdom come! In Jesus' name I pray. Amen.

2.

Jesus Teaches the Kingdom

JESUS WENT from town to town throughout ancient Israel, teaching about the kingdom of God. The Israelites remembered the kingdoms of David and Solomon, and they thought the Messiah's kingdom would be similar. But Jesus exploded their limited understanding by showing that the kingdom of God is a heavenly kingdom, very different from the kingdoms of the world. It's a spiritual kingdom, and it comes by spiritual power.

Jesus shined light into minds and hearts.

"The entrance of your words gives light. It gives understanding to the simple" (Ps. 119:130).

The word of God is the communication of Himself. Through God's word, we know and access God, and we understand spiritual reality. As Jesus taught, he imparted vision about the kingdom of God, making the kingdom of God accessible to humanity once again.

Jesus explained the kingdom of God using parables. Parables are stories which reveal spiritual truth by using everyday objects as symbols. The Bible often uses symbols to teach spiritual truths. The lamb represents Jesus (John 1:29), bread represents the word of God (Matt. 4:4), and water represents the Holy Spirit (John 7:38). When these symbols are rightly interpreted, Jesus' parables can be understood.

Contrary to common belief, Jesus did not use parables to make spiritual truth easier to understand. Instead, he used parables to make spiritual truth inaccessible to those who were not relying on the Holy Spirit.

Jesus said:

> To you it has been given to know the mystery of the kingdom of God; but to those who are outside, all things come in parables, so that seeing they may see and not perceive, and hearing they may hear and not understand. (Mark 4:11-12a)

Jesus spoke in parables in order to shroud the truth of God from those who were relying on themselves. We cannot comprehend spiritual things with our minds alone. We need the Holy Spirit to teach us (John 16:13). No one can save themselves.

In Matthew 13, Jesus described the kingdom of God using seven different parables. Each of these parables reveals the kingdom of God from a slightly different perspective. It's like explaining an elephant from 5 different angles – the trunk, the belly, the ears, the tusks, and the tail. When these pictures are put together, we get a more accurate view of the whole. When these seven different perspectives of the kingdom of God are put together, they give a more complete picture of what God's kingdom is.

(Please note that Matthew uses the words kingdom of God and kingdom of heaven interchangeably - see Matthew 19:23.)

1. The Sower

In the first parable, Jesus says the kingdom of God is like a man sowing seed. The sower scatters seed everywhere, into prepared ground, onto the roadside, on top of a rock, and even among thorns and thistles. It looks like he's wasting the seed because he's sowing it so indiscriminately. The birds pluck away the seeds on the roadside. The seeds on the rock grow for a short time but quickly die. The seeds among the thorns grow into plants that never produce fruit. Only the seeds sown in the good soil grow into healthy plants that produce a harvest.

Jesus interprets the symbols of this parable. He says the sower symbolizes himself. The seed represents the word of the kingdom of God. The birds signify Satan. The thorns represent life's stresses. The four different types of ground represent the four types of people that hear the word of God.

Every individual who has ever heard the gospel falls into one of these four categories:

1. The roadside symbolizes people who hear the word of God but don't understand it. Satan steals the word from them, and they do not become a part of God's kingdom.

2. The rocky place represents those who hear the word of God and initially respond eagerly, but when they face trouble because of following Jesus, they fall away.

3. The thorny place is like people who hear the word of God but are so overwhelmed by concerns like money, security, or social standing that the kingdom cannot grow strong in their lives. They bear no fruit.

4. The good ground signifies those who hear the word of God, believe it, and obey it. They produce varying amounts of fruit for God's kingdom.

Jesus said, "Do you not understand this parable? How then will you understand all the parables?" (Mark 4:13).

This parable is uniquely important. It gives a key to understanding all other parables. It does this by interpreting basic spiritual symbols like the sower, the ground, seed, birds, thorns, and fruit. In addition, this parable reveals the importance of understanding the word of God. Understanding the word of God is the first step to fruitfulness, for when we understand the word of God and believe it, it is planted in our hearts. When we have the word of God inside us, it grows and affects our lives, enabling us to work with God in manifesting his kingdom upon the earth. How we respond to God's word determines our fruitfulness for his kingdom.

The word of God is like a seed of the kingdom because it is the beginning of God's rule in the earth. Like the seed of an apple tree contains the potential of many other apples within it, God's word contains the potential of the kingdom of God. When the word of God is accepted, kingdom potential enters a human heart. When the word of God is obeyed, the potential power of the kingdom of God is released into the world, and the kingdom of God is manifested. The word of God, properly planted, will produce a manifestation of the kingdom of God, just like the seed of an apple, properly planted, will produce many apples.

2. Wheat and Tares

In the second parable, Jesus said the kingdom of God is like a man who sowed wheat in his field. Afterwards, his enemy came at night and sowed tares (weeds that look like wheat) in the same field. Workers alerted the man to what had been done. The man said that the tares should be allowed to grow along with the wheat. At harvest, the reapers would first remove the tares from the field and burn them. Afterwards, the wheat would be gathered and put into the barn.

Jesus says the owner of the field symbolizes himself. The field represents the world, and the wheat seed symbolizes the children of God. The enemy represents Satan, and the tares symbolize Satan's children. The harvest symbolizes the end of the age, and the reapers represent angels.

This parable reveals many truths. First of all, it explains that throughout the world, God's children are growing to fulfill God's purposes. God's word is the incorruptible seed (see 1 Peter 1:23) which causes people to be born again into God's family. False teachings are like evil seeds. Under the cover of darkness, which represents the absence of spiritual light, Satan has put his own children among the children of God by deceiving them through false teachings.

Just as tares look like wheat, it is sometimes hard to distinguish between the children of God and the children of Satan. There are many people in the world who profess to know Jesus, but they don't know him at all. When tares are planted near wheat, their root systems get all tangled up together. False Christians are often connected with the true children of God, participating in church activities and ministries.

The end of the age is harvest time. The timing of the harvest is determined by crop maturity. Only when the grain is ripe can it be harvested. Christians are the spiritual wheat that is currently growing into maturity. Christian growth happens corporately, for each individual grain of wheat is in a head with many other grains of wheat (Mark 4:28), and they all grow together in the field. Only within the body of Christ can individual Christians reach their full potential. Corporate growth will continue "Until we all come in the unity of the faith, and of the knowledge of the Son of God, to a perfect man, to the measure of the stature of the fullness of Christ" (Ephesians 4:13).

A mature grain of wheat looks like the initial seed from which it sprang. Jesus is the initial seed (John 12:24), and Christians are being conformed to his image. When they represent Jesus to the world as he is, then they will become mature. No Christian has yet reached full maturity. Paul was striving for full maturity when he said, "I press on, that I may lay hold of that for which Christ Jesus has also laid hold of me" (Phil. 3:12). Every believer has a calling from God to be like Jesus, and God is waiting for us to fulfill it. When we do, it will be harvest time.

When the wheat matures, so will the tares. Mature tare grains are black. At harvest, it will become obvious that tares are not wheat. At the end of the age, it will be evident that false Christians are not the people of God. The angels will remove the unbelievers from the world and burn them in the fire of God's judgment. After this, the children of God will shine forth brightly in the kingdom of God.

3. The Mustard Seed

The third parable is of the mustard seed.

> He told them another parable: "The kingdom of heaven is like a mustard seed, which a man took and sowed in his field, which indeed is the least of all the seeds, but when it is grown it is greater than the herbs and becomes a tree, so that the birds of the air come and nest in its branches." (Matthew 13:31-32)

The interpretation of this parable, unlike that of the previous two, is not revealed in the Bible. We need to rely on what Jesus had previously taught and on the inspiration of the Holy Spirit in order to understand it.

As with all parables, we must begin by interpreting the symbols. The field symbolizes the world. The owner of the field who planted the seed represents God. The seed signifies Jesus.

Jesus said, "most assuredly, I say to you, unless a grain of wheat falls into the ground and dies, it remains alone; but if it dies, it produces much grain" (John 12:24).

Jesus was talking about himself. He is the "seed of the woman" that was sown into the earth. In this parable, Jesus is compared to a mustard seed. Jesus often used mustard seeds to refer to something small in size (see Luke 17:6). Jesus' life in the earth began in a small way. He was born in a barn, carried the shame of being an illegitimate child (as people thought), and grew up as a carpenter.

When Jesus was about 33 years old, he died on the cross. Then he was buried and figuratively planted in the earth. After he rose up from the dead, the Holy Spirit was poured out upon his disciples, and they were grafted into his body. "We are members of His body, of His flesh, and of His bones" (Ephesians 5:30).

Through the power of resurrection, Christ was transformed into a many-membered body, comprised of everyone who believes in Jesus. "For as the body is one and has many members, but all the members of that one body, being many, are one body, so also is Christ" (1 Corinthians 12:12).

The body of Christ is the church, and it is symbolized by the tree which grew supernaturally from a very small seed. The church, as part of Christ (his body), is called to reveal the kingdom of God to the world. The growth of the kingdom of God in the earth mirrors the growth of the church, for the kingdom of God expands through the ministry of the church. As the church grows in submission to God, so the kingdom of God advances upon the earth.

In this parable, birds came and rested in the branches of the tree. The birds symbolize Satan and his evil spirits, just as they do in the first parable (Matthew 13:4,19). The birds are not part of the tree, but they fly in and sit on its branches. The New Testament warns in multiple places that the church would be affected by demonic forces. Just as in the history of Israel there was often idolatry and worship of the devil, so in the church there is often Satanic deception. Satan infiltrates the church through evil spirits and false teachings which hide among church branches. These demonic incursions hinder the ministry of the church and stunt the growth of God's kingdom.

4. The Leaven

The fourth parable is about the leaven. "Another parable he spoke unto them, 'The kingdom of heaven is like leaven, which a woman took and hid in three measures of meal till it was all leavened'" (Matthew 13:33).

In some parts of the Bible, leaven represents sin or false doctrine. However, in this parable, Jesus says that leaven symbolizes the kingdom of God. Sometimes the Bible uses the same symbols to represent different things, and context must determine the correct interpretation. For example, a lion can symbolize Jesus (Revelation 5:5) or Satan (1 Peter 5:8). The morning star can represent Jesus (Revelation 22:16) or Satan (Isaiah 14:12 in Hebrew). Context and the Holy Spirit determine the correct interpretation of Biblical symbols. In this parable, Jesus said the leaven symbolizes the kingdom of God.

The woman represents the church, as she often does throughout the New Testament (2 Corinthians 11:2, Ephesians 5:23-27). The three measures of flour is a lot of flour, enough to make approximately 52 loaves of bread. The flour symbolizes the world.

The church takes the kingdom of God— Christ's words and works— and puts it into the world in ways that are often hidden and unseen. But the leaven is working, and someday, the kingdom of God will permeate the entire earth. This parable emphasizes both the permeative quality and the totality of the kingdom of God. Someday, the kingdom of God will impact the entire world. This will culminate at Christ's return.

5. The Hidden Treasure

The fifth parable is about treasure hidden in a field. "Again, the kingdom of heaven is like treasure hidden in a field, which a man found and hid, and for joy over it he goes and sells all that he has and buys that field" (Matthew 13:44).

The field symbolizes the world (as in Matthew 13:38). The man who buys the field represents Jesus. The treasure in the field signifies God's people.

Before people believe the gospel, they are hidden in the world, covered over by sin and evil. Jesus saw his people in the midst of the world's grime. Full of love for them and anticipating the joy of being reunited with them for eternity, Jesus symbolically sold all that he had. He laid aside his glory in heaven and came to earth as a baby. Then he went to the cross and died.

Paul explains Christ's emptying:

> [Jesus] made himself of no reputation, taking the form of a bondservant, and coming in the likeness of men. And being found in appearance as a man,

he humbled himself and became obedient to the point of death, even the death of the cross. (Philippians 2:7-8)

Jesus, "for the joy that was set before him endured the cross, despising the shame, and has sat down at the right hand of the throne of God" (Hebrews 12:2).

Jesus bought the world out of the grip of the devil by paying the ultimate price of his own life. When he rose up from the dead, everyone who would ever believe in Jesus rose up together with him, to be united with him forever. Jesus died to rescue us, and fellowship with us is his reward.

6. The Pearl

The sixth parable is the pearl of great price. "Again, the kingdom of heaven is like a merchant seeking beautiful pearls, who, when he had found one pearl of great price, went and sold all that he had and bought it" (Matt. 13:45-46).

This parable, like the previous one, reveals the value of the kingdom of God. But this time its value is revealed not from the perspective of Christ, but from the perspective of a person on earth who finds the kingdom. We are commanded to seek first for the kingdom of

God and his righteousness (Matthew 6:33), above everything else. We must be willing to give up everything in order to gain the kingdom of God. The pearl symbolizes entrance into God's heavenly city, which is described in Revelation as being through a gate made out of a single pearl (Revelation 21:21).

The merchant man is someone who has been trading in the world. He discovers that the kingdom of God is the greatest thing he could possibly find on earth, the one thing that gives meaning and purpose to his life. He gives up all his possessions, and possibly everything else of earthly value (like honor, praise of men, and social standing), in order to gain entrance into the kingdom of God. The Lord will often ask us to take steps of obedience, including the giving away of our possessions, in order to enter into the kingdom of God (see Mark 10:21-23).

This parable emphasizes the fact that the kingdom of God is to be our main priority, just as we are Christ's priority. We must be willing to give up everything in order to become a part of this kingdom. Jesus gave his all for us; we should be willing to give up our all for him.

7. The Net

The seventh and final parable is about the net.

> Again, the kingdom of heaven is like a dragnet that was cast into the sea and gathered some of every kind, which, when it was full, they drew to shore; and sat down and gathered the good into vessels, but threw the bad away. So it will be at the end of the age. The angels will come forth, separate the wicked from among the just, and cast them into the furnace of fire. There will be wailing and gnashing of teeth. (Matthew 13:47-50)

The sea represents the mass of humanity (Revelation 17:15). The net is the kingdom of God, which will eventually cover the world and gather up all kinds of people under God's authority and rule. The end of the age will happen when the net is full, and "the fullness of the Gentiles" (Romans 11:25) have been gathered in.

When the end of the age comes, Jesus will rule over the earth. All people will be brought before his throne for judgment. The wicked will be condemned, separated, and thrown away. Then the righteous will shine forth in God's kingdom.

This parable reveals the totality of the kingdom of God. It's going to swallow up everything and ultimately affect everyone who has ever lived.

. . .

These 7 parables in Matthew give a foundation for understanding the kingdom of God. Jesus spoke other parables about the kingdom, including the parable of the 10 virgins and the parable of the talents. But these 7 parables provide a basic framework for understanding God's kingdom. This basic foundation of Jesus' teaching will prepare us to experience the kingdom of God. This is God's goal.

"For the kingdom of God is not in word but in power" (1 Corinthians 4:20).

- Kingdom Core -

1. Christ came to rescue the creation from darkness and restore the kingdom of God to the world.

2. The kingdom of God is a spiritual kingdom, and it is revealed by spiritual power.

3. God's kingdom is not only for a future time in heaven, but for now, for every nation and every corner of the world.

4. The kingdom of God cost Jesus everything, and it is worth our entire lives.

5. God's kingdom is growing in the earth through the ministry of the church.

6. Satan infiltrates the church with evil spirits and false teachings, hindering the growth of the kingdom of God.

7. Someday, in spite of these challenges, the kingdom of God will take over the world.

8. When mature believers represent Christ accurately upon the earth, it will be the end of the age.

- Prayer -

Dear God, there are so many treasures in your word. Give me a hunger and thirst for your word, and wisdom to understand it. Your kingdom is so great. Thank you for teaching me about your kingdom in so many different ways. Please deliver me from all deception. Open my eyes to understand. It is impossible for me to know about your kingdom through my own mind. I need your Holy Spir-it. Please teach me. In Jesus' name I pray. Amen.

3. Jesus Brings the Kingdom

THE KINGDOM OF GOD is defined by the will of God. Wherever God's will is done, the kingdom of God comes. God's kingdom exists whenever people obey him, and it expands whenever new people submit to him. The kingdom of God is the practical outworking of God's will upon the earth.

Jesus told us to pray for God's kingdom to come and for his will to be done (Matthew 6:10). These two requests are basically one and the same, because whenever God's will is done, his kingdom comes. The accomplishment of God's will on the earth marks the arrival of God's kingdom to the earth.

God's will does not automatically happen. In fact, many of the things that happen in the world are not God's will. For example, it was not God's will for Adam and Eve to eat the forbidden fruit, but they ate it anyway. It is not God's will for you or I to sin, but we still sometimes sin. Since God's will is often not happening, we must seek and pray for God's will to be done.

In order for us to seek first the kingdom of God, which is our life purpose, we must know the will of God. When we know God's will, then we can recognize the boundaries of God's kingdom. We will be able to recognize what is inside God's kingdom and what is outside it. Then we will understand how to live within his kingdom and how to seek for the expansion of his kingdom on the earth.

"Do not be unwise, but understand what the will of the Lord is" (Ephesians 5:17).

Jesus Reveals God's Will

To discover the will of God, we need to look to Jesus. Jesus revealed the will of God through his life and ministry because he did God's will all the time. He was a perfect representative of his Father.

"He who has seen me has seen the Father" (John 14:9b).

1. *God's will is for people to be saved.*

Jesus revealed that God wants people to be saved, to know him, and to be with him forever.

God "will have all men to be saved and to come unto the knowledge of the truth" (1 Timothy 2:4 KJV). God doesn't want anyone to die in their sins and be lost (2 Peter 3:9).

Jesus came to save people. Corrupt government employees, proud Pharisees, prostitutes, insane people – all types of wretched people met God through Jesus. Wherever Jesus went, he offered salvation to everyone, no matter how bad they were. Today, everyone who believes in Jesus is cleansed from their sins and has eternal life.

Not everyone is saved, of course. Many people reject the gospel. But as the kingdom of God expands on the earth, more and more people are going to be saved.

2. *God wants everyone to stop sinning.*

Sin is never God's will. God didn't want Adam to sin, but he sinned anyway. God didn't want Stalin to commit atrocities, but he slaughtered millions. God doesn't want you or me to sin - but sometimes we do.

Jesus came to set people free from the power of sin. He called and empowered people to forsake sin. Tax collectors gave away their wealth, harlots repented and became holy, and rough fishermen became humble servants of God.

Jesus shed his blood to take away all sin.

People still sin today, even all of God's children. But God wants us to grow in holiness, and he wants all sin to be removed from the world. Someday in the fullness of the kingdom of God, there will be no more sin.

3. God wants people to be healed.

Sickness, like all other forms of decay in the world, came in as a result of the Fall. Jesus came to take away all the evil results of the Fall, including sickness and disease. He healed sick people – lepers, paralyzed people, lame people, blind people, deaf people, and dumb people. There was no sickness that was too strong for Jesus. When Jesus was upon the earth, everyone who came to him asking for healing got healed. Sometimes Jesus healed entire towns (Matthew 8:16). He ultimately dealt with all sickness on the cross (compare Matthew 8:16-17 and Isaiah 53:4). People are still being healed today by the power of Jesus.

There is healing for all sickness through the blood of Jesus. However, until the glorious day when Jesus reigns over the entire earth, people continue to get sick, even God's people. Just as sin is not God's will, so sickness is not God's will. However, both sin and sickness still happen because God's kingdom is not here in fullness, and his will is not yet completely done. Yet at the end of the age, God will ultimately rid the world of all sickness and disease, and in the fullness of the kingdom of God, sickness will be gone.

4. God's will is to destroy Satan.

Jesus came to crush Satan's head. He regularly cast out demons. The New Testament gives about 25 examples of exorcisms, and there were probably many more. Each demon-expulsion was a powerful testimony to Christ's superiority over the kingdom of darkness. "If I cast out demons by the Spirit of God, then the kingdom of God is come unto you" (Matt 12:28).

Throughout his ministry, Jesus cast out demons and tied up dark spiritual forces, setting multitudes free. On the cross, Jesus completely destroyed the power of Satan and every evil spirit. He also gave his disciples authority to cast out evil spirits (Luke 10:19).

Evil spirits are still infesting the world today, and they are still being cast out by the power of Jesus' name. The will of God is to destroy the devil, and someday when Satan is thrown into the lake of fire, the full victory of Christ over Satan and evil spirits will be revealed.

5. *God's will is for his people to have enough food and clothing.*

Jesus promised to provide food and clothing to his followers if they seek God's kingdom above everything else (Luke 12:29-31). Jesus multiplied loaves and fish to feed hungry crowds (Mark 6:41), and he still provides miraculously for his people today. He doesn't want his people to lack the basic necessities of life.

In the fullness of the kingdom of God, there will be no lack.

6. *God's will is to destroy death.*

Jesus came to conquer death. He stopped a funeral procession and emptied a coffin (Luke 7:11-16), raided a tomb and brought a dead man out alive (John 11:38-44), and threw mourners out of a house by raising up a dead girl (Mark 5:21-43). Then he rose up from the dead and gave eternal life to his followers.

Someday, in the fullness of the kingdom of God, death will be swallowed up in victory. Death is the last enemy, and someday it will be gone (1 Corinthians 15:26).

7. *God wants righteousness to prevail all over the world.*

Jesus brought righteousness into the world and gave it away freely, turning sinners into saints. Seeking the kingdom of God is the same as seeking righteousness (Matthew 6:33). When something is righteous, God reigns over it. Wherever there is righteousness, there is God's kingdom. Righteousness equals kingdom presence, and as righteousness spreads, so does the kingdom of God.

God wants righteousness to be all over the world, because he wants his kingdom to be all over the world.

Revealing the Kingdom

Jesus always did the will of God. Perfect submission to the Father caused Jesus to constantly live in and manifest the kingdom of God.

"Most assuredly I say to you, the Son can do nothing of himself, but what he sees the Father do; for whatever he does, the Son also does in like manner" (John 5:19).

The first man was Adam. Adam once had unbroken fellowship with God, submitting to God completely, and on that basis he ruled the world. But Adam sinned and was separated from God, and therefore he could no longer represent the kingdom of God to the world.

"The second man is the Lord from heaven" (1 Corinthians 15:47b).

The second man was Jesus. Jesus never sinned. Through obedience to the Father, Jesus recovered the spiritual power that Adam had lost. Through obedience, Jesus brought the kingdom of God back to the world.

Jesus spoke kingdom words. All his words were straight from God.

"The words I speak unto you, they are spirit and they are life" (John 6:63).

When the Pharisees sent officers to arrest Jesus, they couldn't nab him because his words were too powerful. The officers went back to the Pharisees, explaining that they couldn't capture Jesus for "no man ever spoke like this man" (John 7:46).

Jesus did kingdom works. Everything he did originated in his Father. Whenever someone saw Jesus do something, he saw God do it, because Jesus did whatever the Father did. The Father moved on the earth through the Son. There was no separation between the Father and the Son because the Son always obeyed the Father.

This is why Jesus brought the kingdom wherever he went. Whenever Jesus came to a town, he declared, "The kingdom of heaven is at hand!" (Matt. 4:17). The kingdom had come because Jesus had come. Jesus was inside the kingdom of God, and wherever he went, he brought the kingdom of God.

The secret of Jesus' spiritual strength was his union with his Father. Jesus said, "I and my Father are one" (John 10:30). Because of his perfect union with the Father, Jesus was full of the Holy Spirit, and he radiated divine power into the earth. Jesus not only taught the kingdom; he brought the kingdom. He went from town to town in ancient Israel, doing the will of God. He shook the earth with a revelation of heaven, astounding the world with God's power. He was a point of heavenly light upon the earth, breaking up the dominion of darkness wherever he went. He saved the lost, healed the sick, cast out demons, forgave sin, provided food for the hungry, and raised the dead.

Jesus was clothed with divine authority and anointed with supreme spiritual power. He restored a vision of *God's present rule upon the earth* that had all but disappeared with Eden. Jesus showed that it is possible for the will of God to be done, and for the kingdom of God to come. He proved that God's kingdom can take over the world.

The Devil Strikes Back

Not surprisingly, Satan hated Jesus and his kingdom revelation. When Jesus was born, the devil inspired Herod to murder all the male babies in Bethlehem in a desperate attempt to kill the Christ. A timely dream to Joseph caused the young family to flee just in time.

Right before Jesus' public ministry began, Satan assaulted him in the desert. Jesus was hungry, thirsty, and tired, and Satan approached him through twisted applications of the word of God. But Jesus rejected the devil's lies and emerged victorious.

Throughout Jesus' ministry, Satan attacked him through slander, mobs, and full-on assault. It was all to no avail, and Jesus won every time.

Christ is the eternal God— the creator of the world, the Lord of heaven, and Almighty in power. Although he laid aside this great glory to come to the earth as a man, he was not weak. Jesus Christ was perfect and holy, filled with the Holy Spirit, in constant fellowship with God, and backed up by the armies of heaven.

The Final Assault

Jesus' ministry culminated when he came to Jerusalem in a triumphant, joyful procession, riding into the Holy City. The excited crowd shouted "Hosanna!" and threw their coats on the road before him. They waved palm branches in celebration. They finally recognized that Jesus was the Messiah.

Satan probably figured that if he didn't somehow stop him now, Jesus would take over the world. Satan marshaled all his forces for a final assault against the Son of God. He instigated Jesus' own treasurer to turn against him. Judas shared a final meal with Jesus and then went out into the dark night and turned him in. An armed mob came hunting for Jesus with sanction from the government.

God-as-man was arrested by those who claimed to be his children. He was dragged before the rulers. A demonized religious system hurled false accusations and slander at Jesus, calling him the devil. He was blamed for real crimes, but not those committed by him. According to the religious leaders, Jesus was a rebel against God and man. Little did they know that in condemning him, they were condemning themselves. All the crimes of humanity from the history of the world that had ever been committed against God were laid on Jesus Christ.

Jesus was convicted while Barabbas, the real murderer and rebel, went free.

Jesus was led to the place of execution by the Roman State. They nailed his hands and feet to a cross and hoisted him up between earth and heaven. Dying, in physical agony, Jesus was separated from his Father for the first time in his life. All the sins that had ever been committed in the history of the world were laid on him. Even God seemed to reject him. Struggling and gasping for breath, he suffocated under this terrible weight of sin and died.

With Jesus dead, the powerful kingdom of God that had been sweeping through Israel like wildfire suddenly came to a screeching halt. There were no salvations, healings, resurrections, or deliverances.

The King of the Jews hung lifeless on a cross with nails piercing his hands and feet. Darkness shrouded the holy city.

It seemed as though the ancient serpent had won.

Christ's dead body was taken down from the cross, carried away, and laid in a rock tomb. The cave was covered with a huge stone, sealed shut, and guarded by soldiers.

Christ's disciples wept and ran away in fear.

His enemies gloated.

Jesus went down into hell with all the evil of the world on his back. Satan threw his worst at him. All the sins of the world were laid upon him, and every sickness, disease, and curse was put upon him. Powerful fallen angels attacked him. Demons pounded at him. He tasted death for every person who ever lived.

Christ's heel was bruised. But it was bruised in the process of stamping on Satan's head, smashing it to pieces forever.

Resurrection

Up, through the depths of hell,
Up, through the hordes of darkness,
Up, through the terrible load of the sins of the world
Came Christ.

Jesus threw off everything everywhere that ever had been or ever would be contrary to God. He demolished every sin that had ever been committed by anyone anywhere in the world at any time. He broke every curse, shattered every witchcraft, and defeated every sickness. Christ broke through the gates of hell, came back to the earth, re-entered his physical body, and brought it back to life. On the morning of the third day, the glory of God began to shine in the dark cave where his body had been buried, and Jesus burst forth as a powerful spiritual conqueror who had defeated every enemy and stripped all the forces of darkness of their power.

Jesus had won. He had accomplished all that needed to be done in order to restore God's kingdom to the world. He dealt with sin and all its evil effects, taking away not only the sin of Adam, but taking away every sin of everyone— past, present, or future. By conquering sin, Jesus conquered all the evil results of sin— every demon, every curse, every sickness, and all decay. The defeat of every enemy and the freedom of every slave was purchased by his shed blood.

Finally, after millennia of darkness, the devil's power was broken, and the kingdom of God could come flooding into the world again.

If Jesus had wanted to, he could have lived on the earth forever, going from nation to nation, setting up his kingdom as he astounded the world with heaven's miracles and glory. No President could have resisted him, and no army could have stopped him. From his headquarters somewhere in the earth, Jesus might have established an earthly kingdom, resolving all disputes and reigning by the irresistible force of divine authority.

But Jesus had a different plan. He taught his apostles for 40 days about the kingdom of God, giving "commandments to the apostles whom He had chosen…being seen by them during forty days and speaking of the things pertaining to the kingdom of God" (Acts 1:3b). This extensive teaching to the apostles laid the foundation for their teachings about church and other vital aspects of the kingdom of God that are revealed throughout the Book of Acts and the Epistles.

Then, after giving these important teachings, Jesus rose up to heaven and sat down at the right hand of God.

"From henceforth expecting till his enemies be made his footstool" (Hebrews 10:13 KJV).

— *Kingdom Core* —

1. Jesus Christ came to restore God's kingdom to the world.

2. Whenever God's will is done, his kingdom comes.

3. Jesus did God's will perfectly, revealing the kingdom of God wherever he went.

4. Jesus defeated sin, thereby removing all evil.

5. Through death and resurrection, Jesus defeated Satan and every enemy of God, and bought the right for the kingdom of God to rule over the entire earth again.

— *Prayer* —

Jesus, thank you for coming to this earth and shedding your blood to take away my sins and the sins of the whole world. I praise you that you did the will of God perfectly, revealing the amazing extent of God's love as you ministered on the earth. Help me to believe that God's will can come to pass on this earth. Forgive me for the times I have been slow to believe in you. You are a mighty conqueror. You are a glorious king. You have destroyed every enemy, and because of you, the kingdom of God is going to take over the world. Praise you both now and forever! Amen.

4.

Christians Bring the Kingdom

As the Father has sent me, I also send you.

John 20:21b

EARLY IN HIS MINISTRY, Jesus anointed 12 disciples with the Holy Spirit, giving them spiritual power to reveal the kingdom of God (Matthew 10:1-8). The 12 apostles preached the gospel, healed the sick, and cast out demons.

Later, Jesus anointed 70 more disciples with spiritual power, and they began revealing the kingdom of God (Luke 10:1-20).

After his resurrection, Jesus poured out the Holy Spirit on 120 disciples in the Upper Room. Filled with the fire of God, they burst into Jerusalem, releasing the power of God's kingdom. On the day of Pentecost, 120 people quickly became 5,000, as multitudes believed the gospel and joined the church. Daily, more and more people were added, and the kingdom of God was expanding rapidly on the earth.

The Body of Christ

Jesus' body had risen up from the dead and had become the many-membered body of Christ (1 Corinthians 12:12). Since that time, all who believe in Jesus become part of his body.

"For we are members of his body, of his flesh and of his bones" (Ephesians 5:30).

With the incorporation of so many people into the body of Christ, the ministry of Jesus was no longer confined to one man. Each believer was filled with the same Holy Spirit that empowered Jesus, and Christ's "body parts" were bringing the kingdom of God into many places on the earth simultaneously. Paul went throughout the Mediterranean, Thomas went to India, and other disciples went to other far-flung regions, preaching the kingdom of God.

The church was continuing the ministry that Jesus began. Lost people were saved, sick people were healed, demons were expelled, and dead people were raised. The body of Christ was standing on the earth in a sense where Jesus had stood, representing God's kingdom to the world.

"Most assuredly, I say to you, he who believes in me, the works that I do, he will do also; and greater works than these he will do, because I go to my Father" (John 14:12).

There is no limit to the spiritual power that can be unleashed through the church. Jesus said with assurance that we would do greater works than he did.

Jesus was a Master of the spirit realm, and we are called to be like him by the Holy Spirit. "Everyone who is perfectly trained will be like his master" (Luke 6:40). As we grow into the likeness of our Master Jesus, we will be increasingly able to dominate for his kingdom the way our humble Master did.

The Internal Kingdom

We enter the kingdom of God the moment we are born again. "He has delivered us from the power of darkness, and conveyed us into the kingdom of the Son of his love" (Colossians 1:13).

When we are born again, our spirits are united to Jesus (1 Corinthians 6:17), and our bodies become "temples of the Holy Spirit" (1 Corinthians 6:19). When we are baptized in the Holy Spirit, we are filled with the Holy Spirit for the first time and empowered to be God's witnesses (Acts 1:8). The indwelling Holy Spirit is the internal deposit of the kingdom of God.

Jesus said, "the kingdom of God is within you" (Luke 17:21b).

Stupendous spiritual power resides inside each Christian. The Holy Spirit has already conquered all evil by raising up Jesus from the dead. The resurrection proves that the Holy Spirit can reverse all the effects of the Fall, because He has already conquered them all. There is no sin stronger than the power of the Holy Spirit, no demon that can't be defeated by the Holy Spirit, and no sickness stronger than the Holy Spirit. May we know "the exceeding greatness of His power toward us who believe, according to the working of His mighty power which He worked in Christ when He raised Him from the dead" (Ephesians 1:19).

"Now to Him who is able to do exceedingly abundantly above all that we ask or think, according to the power that works in us..." (Ephesians 3:20).

The Land of the Soul

The Bible compares our souls to land (Matthew 13:1-23). Our souls are to be occupied by God. They are to be sown with the seed of God's word and filled with the water of the Holy Spirit. Jesus said, "In your patience possess your souls" (Luke 21:19). The Holy Spirit is to dwell in the entirety of our souls, dominating every aspect of our inner man. This includes our minds (thoughts), our hearts (desires), and our emotions. To the extent that we possess our souls, to that extent we can yield our souls to God, and His kingdom can dwell within us. The more our souls are filled with God, the more we can manifest His kingdom to the world.

Hearing From God

Hearing from God is essential to expanding His kingdom. God has crafted unique plans for each of His children, like a specific place for us to live, words for us to speak, and tasks for us to accomplish. These specific instructions are usually not found within the pages of the Bible, but they are part of the plans God has prepared for each of us from the foundation of the world (Ephesians 2:10). We will discover these specific plans as we hear God's voice.

How will we hear God speak to us? The ability to hear from God comes from the Bible. Studying and obeying God's word opens our ears to hear God speak to us now. As we read and obey the Bible, we get in tune with our heavenly Father, and we gain the ability to hear God's voice more clearly. "Hearing comes by the word of God" (Romans 10:17).

Hearing God is to be normal for every Christian. Jesus said, "My sheep hear my voice, and I know them, and they follow me" (John 10:27).

If we want to see God's kingdom come through us, we must hear accurately from God. We don't want to be deceived by our own minds, by the world, or by the devil. We want to be clear as to what God is actually saying.

How can we know that God is speaking now? Here are 7 keys to hearing accurately from God.

1. Obey the Bible. The commands of Christ and his apostles in the New Testament are perfect instructions that apply to all of God's children. These words provide the form and function of the kingdom of God. When we obey these instructions, we get into the spiritual place where God can speak to us more specifically. Obeying these general commands is essential to receiving more revelation. But if we do not obey the general instructions in the Bible, God may not speak more specifically to us.

2. Test everything by the Bible. God will not speak anything to us that is contrary to the Bible. If a "word" contradicts the Bible, throw it out.

3. Test things with mature Christians. God can speak to us through other members in the body of Christ. Let's be humble to receive words God may speak to us through our brothers and sisters. Furthermore, mature believers can be used by God to confirm or deny words that we think we've heard from God. Let's avail ourselves of the valuable spiritual resources within the body of Christ.

4. Obey current revelation. As we obey God's words, he will give us further instructions. But if we are not doing

what God has already told us to do, he may not give us further instructions.

5. Patience. It takes time to hear God's voice. As we wait, we need to pray, read the Bible, and have fellowship with mature believers. Discernment may take time. If we feel God may have spoken something to us, but we are not sure, we should wait. If the word is from God, it will become obvious over time. Furthermore, after we have received a word from God, it may take time for that word to come to pass. We need to wait for God's word to happen. For all these things, we need patience.

6. Handle mistakes well. As we learn to hear from God, we might make mistakes. Maybe we think God is saying something he isn't, or maybe we miss his voice when he is speaking. Mistakes are part of growing up. Every child makes mistakes when they learn to walk; these mistakes are not a sign that the child should give up learning to walk. We should not give up spiritually when we make mistakes. Instead, we keep learning to walk by the Spirit. If you make a mistake, learn from it. Apologize to others who may have been affected by the mistake. Stay in the Bible, keep in fellowship with mature Christians, and continue learning to listen to God.

7. Be humble. None of us are infallible. We need humility as we wait for God to confirm or deny words that we may believe are from him. Humility is particularly important when we think God has given us a word for someone else. Humbly present your "word from God" to your brother or sister: "I think God might be saying this, but I'm not sure. Please pray and see if he speaks the same thing to you." Humility is essential for a servant of God.

As we learn to hear God's voice, we will learn to reveal his kingdom, for the kingdom comes into the earth through those who obey him.

— *Kingdom Core* —

1. Jesus rose up from the dead and became the head of the body of Christ. The body of Christ (the church) is continuing Christ's ministry of restoring the kingdom of God to the world.

2. Everyone who is born again is inside the kingdom of God now.

3. The kingdom of God is within God's people because the Holy Spirit is inside them.

4. As the Holy Spirit dominates our souls, the kingdom potential within us increases.

5. Obeying the King unleashes the Kingdom.

6. As Christians learn to hear God's voice more clearly, they will become more powerful revealers of God's kingdom.

— *Prayer* —

Heavenly Father, thank you for the blood of Jesus, which is strong enough to restore your kingdom to the world. Thank you for making me a part of your body. Open my eyes to see the rich spiritual inheritance I have in Jesus, and teach me how to tap into these infinite resources. Help me to hear from you and walk in the Spirit, being sensitive to your leading. In Jesus' name, I pray. Amen.

5.
Kingdom Battles

OUR SPIRITUAL PASSPORT is changed when we become born again. At the moment of regeneration, we become citizens of the kingdom of God (Philippians 3:20). We are citizens of heaven, living in a foreign country called "the world."

"We are of God, and the whole world lies under the sway of the wicked one" (1 John 5:19b).

The world is under the power of the devil. It is not our home. Heaven is our home.

Kingdom Ambassadors

Christians are ambassadors of the kingdom of God. "Now then, we are ambassadors for Christ, as though

God were pleading through us; we implore you on Christ's behalf, be reconciled to God" (2 Corinthians 5:20).

An ambassador is "a diplomatic official of the highest rank appointed and accredited as representative in residence by one government or sovereign to another, usually for a specific length of time" (*American Heritage Dictionary*). Ambassadors live in a foreign country, representing their home country to that foreign country. An ambassador seeks the interests of his home country within the country he lives in. The government of his home country tells him what to say and do, and grants him authority. As he follows the orders of his home country, he operates under the authority of his home country, and he remains under his home country's protection.

As Christians, as long as we are stationed in the foreign country of the world, we are ambassadors of God's kingdom. We are to seek the interests of God's kingdom and follow God's orders. As we represent the interests of God's kingdom in the world, we will be protected by God's power.

Kingdom Soldiers

We are not only ambassadors, but we are soldiers. Kingdoms expand as they defeat their enemies and take over new territory. The kingdom of God grows as the devil's works are destroyed, and the Holy Spirit wins. As soldiers, we enter into spiritual battles whenever we do things like share the truth of God's word, pray for people, cast out demons, obey God, or encourage others to obey God. These are all opportunities for God's kingdom to defeat its enemies and expand.

We are called to be good soldiers of Jesus Christ (2 Timothy 2:3) who "fight the good fight of faith" (1 Timothy 6:12). God is looking for effective soldiers who will array heavenly artillery against the devil's fortresses, tearing down Satan's castles and releasing captives.

Our authority in this spiritual war comes from Jesus Christ.

> All authority has been given to Me in heaven and on earth. Go therefore and make disciples of all the nations, baptizing them in the name of the Father and of the Son and of the Holy Spirit, teaching them to observe all things that I have commanded you; and

lo, I am with you always, even to the end of the age.
(Matthew 28:18b-20)

Jesus gave us marching orders. Make disciples of all nations. Teach them to obey everything he commanded in
the New Testament. Let everyone know that Jesus has
conquered. Satan is defeated, and sin is destroyed. Tell
the world, "You can live forever through Jesus Christ!
Turn away from darkness and toward the light of God.
Obey Jesus and live a new life as a part of his kingdom.
There is victory in the name of Jesus over the forces of
darkness!"

Winning Some and Losing Some

We're on the winning side in this great war. But we're
not going to win every spiritual battle. One day we'll
share the gospel and see a soul saved, but other times
people will reject the gospel. Sometimes we'll pray and
sick people will be healed, but other times they won't be
healed.

Why do God's soldiers sometimes lose spiritual battles?
There are three main reasons why we might lose.

1. Free will. When we seek to advance the kingdom of
God, we are ministering to people. And people have free
will. Sometimes people choose to follow God, and some-

times they don't want to follow him. Sometimes they submit to his word, and sometimes they rebel. When people choose not to follow God, the kingdom of God will not advance in their lives. God won't force people to choose him, and neither should we. Even Jesus himself was hindered in manifesting God's kingdom when people rejected him. If the people we are ministering to choose to reject God, we may lose kingdom battles.

2. Lack of faith. Once the disciples couldn't cast out a demon because they lacked faith (Matthew 17:19-20). This can happen to us too. If we don't believe God's word, we probably won't see God work. Other times, we may have faith, but the people we are ministering to might lack faith. Once Jesus was unable to do miracles in a place because of the unbelief of the people there (Matthew 13:58). God operates on the basis of faith. If someone believes God's word, it will happen. If someone doesn't believe God's word, it won't happen. Lack of faith can cause the loss of kingdom battles.

3. Sin. Sin can hinder us from operating in the kingdom of God. When we sin, we may lack spiritual strength as we grieve the Holy Spirit. Then we may not prevail in a spiritual battle. When people we are ministering to sin,

God may not work among them until they repent. Sin can cause the loss of spiritual battles.

These three reasons - free will, unbelief, and sin - can cause the loss of kingdom battles. There are other reasons for loss too - maybe the timing is not right, or we need further directions from God. But sometimes we simply don't know why we lose. We may think we've done everything right, and the people we're ministering to seem to be right with God. Yet the devil still seems to win.

Let's not make the mistake of blaming God for these losses. These losses are never God's fault. God is perfect, and he never makes mistakes.

> Indeed, we count them blessed who endure. You have heard of the perseverance of Job and seen the end intended by the Lord - that the Lord is very compassionate and merciful. (James 5:11)

God turned things around for Job, and he can turn things around for us. No matter what happens, even if we lose a battle, God is good, and he loves us.

"In the world you shall have tribulation, but be of good cheer, I have conquered the world," said Jesus (John 16:33b).

Jesus already won it all. Through him, we are more than conquerors. We may lose a few spiritual battles, but we will win the war. And even if we lose, God can bring good out of that.

"And we know that all things work together for good to those who love God, to those who are the called according to his purpose" (Romans 8:28).

Eternal Victory Revealed in Time

We overcome Satan by the blood of the Lamb (Revelation 12:11). Jesus' blood was shed before the foundation of the world (Revelation 13:8). His blood is eternal, transcending time. Although Christ's blood was shed 2,000 years ago on the cross, its power is not confined to any one point in time. It stands over history and can touch all points of history at once. Christ's blood is the eternal fountain of redemption on the earth, from the Fall of Adam to the end of the age.

The blood of Christ was effective in the Old Testament, serving as the reason for the salvation of Old Testament saints. The animal sacrifices of the Old Testament symbolized Christ's death on the cross. By participating in these sacrifices, people demonstrated their faith in God, thereby releasing the power of Christ's blood into their lives.

Today, 2,000 years after the cross, Christ's blood is still effective. The blood of Christ secures the inheritance of the church, making Christ's riches freely available to all who believe. Part of this inheritance includes complete victory over evil. The church is called to manifest Christ's victory to the world. The church reveals Christ's victory by seeing her inheritance in Christ, which is revealed in God's word, and then, by obeying God's word, the church brings the eternal riches of Christ into the earth. Obedience pivots spiritual realities from eternity into time. It brings heaven into the earth. As the church brings the riches of Christ into the earth, the kingdom of God grows upon the earth.

A Growing Kingdom

The kingdom of God began on earth when Jesus Christ was born 2,000 years ago, and it has been growing ever since. God's kingdom will keep growing until it takes over everything.

> For unto us a child is born, unto us a son is given, and the government will be upon his shoulder…of the increase of his government and peace there shall be no end. (Isaiah 9:6-7)

The child is Christ. The government is the kingdom of God. Isaiah prophesied that Christ's kingdom would continue increasing forever, until it takes over the entire universe. Nothing can stop this inevitable victory.

Even when the Antichrist is raging and breaking down the earth, the kingdom of God will continue growing inexorably. Eventually, there will be no part of the earth that is not under the kingdom of God. Even after Jesus returns, the kingdom of God will continue expanding forever as he unfolds his infinite riches to his creatures throughout eternity.

— *Kingdom Core* —

1. The kingdom of God advances on the earth through revelations of spiritual power.

2. We are ambassadors who represent the kingdom of God to the world.

3. We are soldiers who fight spiritual battles for the advancement of God's kingdom.

4. The kingdom of God is currently growing on the earth and will keep growing throughout eternity.

5. We may lose some spiritual battles, but we will ultimately win the war. We should not be discouraged.

6. Christ's eternal blood guarantees the ultimate victory of the kingdom of God.

7. The growth of the kingdom of God upon the earth is a process of the eternal riches of Christ being manifested in time.

— *Prayer* —

Heavenly Father, I want to be a channel through whom your kingdom can come into the world. Let my faith rise above past discouragements. You are the eternal victor, and nothing can stop the ultimate triumph of your kingdom. Strengthen me to boldly enter into battles you call me to, and may your power prevail. Help me to believe in your kingdom's current progress and inevitable triumph. In Jesus' name I pray. Amen.

6.

Kingdom Politics

GUNS AND BOMBS are the violent tools of political power, but they are worthless for God's reign. When a mob came to Gethsemane to arrest Jesus, Peter drew a sword and cut off someone's ear. Jesus picked up the lopped-off ear and reattached it, showing that the carnal weapons of the state have no part in his revolution. Then Jesus showed real power. He spoke a few words and the entire mob staggered to the ground.

We read about this interesting event in the gospel of John.

> Then Judas, having received a detachment of troops, and officers from the chief priests and Pharisees, came there with lanterns, torches, and weapons. Je-

sus therefore, knowing all things that would come upon Him, went forward and said to them, "Whom are you seeking?" They answered Him, "Jesus of Nazareth." Jesus said to them, "I am He." And Judas, who betrayed Him, also stood with them. Now when He said to them, "I am He," they drew back and fell to the ground. (John 18:3-6)

Presumably, Jesus could have used this heavenly power to do more than knock over a mob. He could have disarmed the officers, preventing his arrest. He might have become invisible and escaped their grasp. He could have been translocated across town à la Philip (Acts 8:39-40). However, he chose not to employ any of these options. Instead, he permitted the mob to rise up from the ground, unharmed. Then they arrested him. Jesus yielded like a lamb to his shearers, so he could die for our sins.

"The kingdom of God is not in word, but in power" (1 Corinthians 4:20).

Jesus proved that the Holy Spirit is stronger than earthly weapons. The same Holy Spirit that knocked down the mob in Gethsemane resides within us.

"The weapons of our warfare are not carnal, but mighty in God for pulling down strongholds" (2 Corinthians 10:4).

Carnal weapons, which are physical and dependent on the flesh, are limited to the material realm. In contrast, spiritual weapons are mediated by the Holy Spirit and far surpass the capabilities of material weapons such as guns and bombs. Divine spiritual weapons can impact the spiritual or material realm without any limit. God and the heavenly hosts are stronger than any nation's armies.

Christians do not require carnal, material weapons to advance God's kingdom. A Christian militia equipped with the latest rifles and artillery will not be able to advance God's kingdom. We have a power that is greater than these things.

Just as carnal weapons can't advance God's kingdom, so modern political methods are useless for God's kingdom. Even if Christians were to mobilize the United States' electorate so that Christians control the Presidency, both houses of Congress, as well as the Supreme Court, the kingdom of God would not come any faster than if Jesus had taken over Rome from Caesar.

Uniting church and state doesn't work. Back in the 4th century, the Roman Emperor Constantine supposedly converted to Christianity and united the church with the Roman Empire. Not long after this, the Emperor decreed that everyone throughout the Roman Empire must worship Jesus Christ alone. Such a decree may have sounded good to some Christians at the time, but this ecclesiastical-political combination led to disaster. The church became a human political organization that relied on the force of man's laws and the soldiers of the state. Every baby in the Roman Empire became a "Christian" by virtue of simply being born, and the church became full of Christians who were Christians in name only, not in heart. Pagan rituals invaded the church, and sin abounded. The Roman Catholic "church" persecuted true believers in Jesus and drove them underground. This "church" became one of the bloodiest organizations on earth, torturing and burning people alive throughout the thousand-year period of the Dark Ages.

The union between church and state didn't work well in the past, and it won't work better in the future. The tools and systems of human political power are incompatible with God's reign. God does not require carnal weapons or human political systems to advance his kingdom.

These things are insufficient for God's reign. God's kingdom is "not of this world" (John 18:36). It operates in a completely different way and is based on superior power than the kingdoms of the world. God is not interested in ruling the earth through human governments.

Submit to Governments

Although human governments are, in many ways, incompatible with the kingdom of God, we are not called to rebel against them. Jesus submitted to human governments (Matthew 17:24-27), and he tells us to submit to them too.

"Let every soul be subject to the governing authorities. For there is no authority except from God, and the authorities that exist are appointed by God" (Romans 13:1). (See the *Appendix* for how evil authorities can be ordered by God.)

"Render therefore to all their due: taxes to whom taxes are due, customs to whom customs, fear to whom fear, honor to whom honor" (Romans 13:7).

The Bible tells us to pray for and thank God for our political leaders.

Therefore I exhort first of all that supplications, prayers, intercessions, and giving of thanks be made for all men, for kings and all who are in authority, that we may lead a quiet and peaceable life in all godliness and reverence. (1 Timothy 2:1-2)

There are many paradoxes in the relationship between human governments and God's kingdom. Earthly governments are fundamentally incompatible with God's kingdom, yet Christians are commanded to submit to them. Christians are to seek the expansion of God's government on earth until all human governments cease to exist, yet we are called to submit to human governments while they still do exist. Human governments often promote horrible evil, but we are not called to rebel against them. The wicked Emperor Nero murdered Christians and ravaged the church, yet Paul told the Christians in Rome under Nero's reign to submit to him.

To better understand all this, we need to learn about the spiritual basis of human governments.

The Prince of This World

The current political ruler over the world is the devil. Jesus called Satan "the prince of this world" (John 14:30

KJV). In calling Satan "prince," Jesus recognized the devil's political power.

How did Satan become in charge of world politics? In the beginning, Adam had governmental power over the earth. But at the Fall, Adam handed the world's political power to Satan. Now he still has this political power, and he gives it to whomever he desires. The following passage reveals this.

> Then the devil, taking Him up on a high mountain, showed Him all the kingdoms of the world in a moment of time. And the devil said to Him, "All this authority I will give You, and their glory; for this has been delivered to me, and I give it to whomever I wish. Therefore, if You will worship before me, all will be Yours." (Luke 4:5-7)

This passage shows that the political power of the world was given to Satan at the Fall, and he gives this power to whomever he desires.

Jesus came to wrest this power back from the devil by crushing his head. When Jesus went to the cross, Satan was eternally "cast out" from his dominion over the world (John 12:31). This eternal "casting out" was completed once for all by Christ's death and resurrection.

However, like other aspects of Christ's victory, this "casting out" is currently in the process of being manifested to the world. Until this victory is fully revealed, Satan remains essentially in charge of world politics.

Principalities and Powers

The devil rules the world through fallen angels. The Bible calls these evil rulers "principalities and powers."

> For we do not wrestle against flesh and blood, but against principalities, against powers, against the rulers of the darkness of this age, against spiritual hosts of wickedness in the heavenly places. (Ephesians 6:12)

The Bible says the principalities and powers are located in heaven. In heaven, they hold spiritual positions of power over the earth. It's important for us as Christians to understand heaven. Heaven is a place of spiritual power that controls the earth. When God created the universe, he also created thrones and dominions in heaven. These invisible, heavenly thrones are spiritual seats of power that control the earth (Colossians 1:16). The principalities and powers (fallen angels) currently sit on these heavenly thrones from which they dominate the nations. God is on the highest throne, but these spirits are on lower thrones that dominate the earth. They gained a right to be on these thrones due to the Fall.

Kings and queens of nations have traditionally believed that their royal power derived from the "gods." Divine-human connections were the basis of the divine right of kings to rule. Royalty has interacted with (or claimed to interact with) fallen angels throughout history. Archaeological discoveries reveal such interactions between them in almost all ancient cultures.

The principalities and powers hold dominion over human governments (Judges 11:24; 1 Kings 11:33). Each nation seems to have its own fallen angel that dominates its affairs. For example, the prince of Persia was a fallen angel who ruled over the kingdom of Persia, and the prince of Greece was a fallen angel who dominated the kingdom of Greece (Daniel 10:13, 20).

Jesus stripped the principalities and powers of their authority on the cross (Colossians 2:15). All fallen angels have eternally lost their power. However, like other aspects of Christ's eternal victory, this victory over fallen angels is not yet fully revealed in time. Therefore, Christians must "wrestle" (Ephesians 6:12) against fallen angels as they seek to expand God's kingdom upon the earth.

Spiritual Solutions for Political Problems

Jesus was fully aware that earthly political systems are sustained by dark spiritual forces, which is why he did not confront human political leaders. Skirmishing with politicians would have been a waste of his time. Jesus focused on defeating the devil, rather than overthrowing Caesar.

> If I with the finger of God cast out demons, no doubt the kingdom of God has come upon you. When a strong man armed keeps his palace, his goods are in peace. But when a stronger one than he shall come upon him and overcome him, he takes from him all his armor wherein he trusted and divides his spoils. (Luke 11:21-22)

In this parable, the strong man represents Satan, and the strong man's possessions represent people, groups, and nations. Jesus is stronger than the strong man; he conquered Satan through superior spiritual power. This victory ultimately freed the nations from the devil's grip. Now Jesus calls the church to walk out his victory by casting out evil spirits like he did.

> Behold, I give unto you power to trample on serpents and scorpions, and over all the power of the

enemy, and nothing shall by any means hurt you. (Luke 10:19)

Christ didn't instruct his apostles to rebel against Herod, but to cast out demons.

Toppling Principalities and Powers

Ultimately, the church is called to confront fallen angels. "To the intent that now unto the principalities and powers in heavenly places might be known by the church the manifold wisdom of God" (Ephesians 3:10). The principalities and powers will be deposed by the power of the word of God declared through the church. The church is not called to rage against fallen angels with loud shouts of rebuke (2 Peter 2:10; Jude 8). Instead, as we submit to Jesus and his authority is revealed through us by Spirit-inspired words and actions, the principalities and powers will be rendered impotent, and their subjection to God will be obvious. When we walk in step with God, we are over these spirits, and nothing will be able to stop us.

At the end of the age, when the church grows into maturity, the lying power of the fallen angels will be exposed, and they will no longer be able to dominate the world. As this happens, the superior power of the Holy

Spirit will knock down the principalities and powers from their heavenly places of power.

The Book of Revelation symbolically describes the principalities and powers falling down from their heavenly thrones as stars falling from heaven, or as figs falling from a fig tree.

> And the stars of heaven fell to the earth, as a fig tree drops its late figs when it is shaken by a mighty wind. Then the sky receded as a scroll when it is rolled up, and every mountain and island was moved out of its place. (Revelation 6:13-14)

Someday soon, evil angels will fall from their thrones of authority by the powerful gusts of the Holy Spirit, and the old heavens will pass away.

> All the host of heaven shall be dissolved, and the heavens shall be rolled up like a scroll; all their host shall fall down as the leaf falls from the vine, and as fruit falling from a fig tree. (Isaiah 34:4)

Isaiah describes the falling of the principalities and powers as dried leaves falling from a vine or dead fruit falling from a tree. He says the passing away of the old heavens will be sudden, like an ancient scroll snapping together when the reading is complete.

When the old heavens pass away, it will greatly affect the earth. The earth will tremble and shake. Nations will be in a tumult. Governments will fall. When the evil spiritual rulers of the world fall, earthly human governments will automatically pass away. When the principalities and powers fall, the human political rulers of the world will no longer be able to rule, for the spiritual basis of their power will have been removed. Without this spiritual power to uphold them, kings and princes will run and hide.

> And the kings of the earth, the great men, the rich men, the commanders, the mighty men, every slave and every free man, hid themselves in the caves and in the rocks of the mountains. (Revelation 6:15)

When the heavens are changed, the earth will also be changed. Thus the heavens and earth will both pass away. When the old heavens and the old earth pass away, a new heavens and a new earth will be created. The corruption of the old world will be gone, and righteousness and peace will dominate the earth. In the new heavens, the saints of God will sit on the heavenly thrones ruling and reigning with Christ (Luke 19:17;

Revelation 20:4). The invisible heavenly thrones and dominions will be occupied by the people of God who will reign over the earth. Then the kingdom of God will be everywhere.

"And he that overcomes, and keeps my works unto the end, to him will I give authority over the nations" (Revelation 2:26).

At the end of the age, the kingdom of God will finally dominate the world politically. Jesus will rule over all nations, and his people will rule with him. The eternal political victory that Christ won on the cross will finally be revealed.

Global Government

Immediately prior to this, there will be great darkness. The Bible tells us that at the end of the age, human governments will unite to form one global government. This single global government will become the worst tyranny the world has ever seen, and it "shall devour the whole earth, trample it down, and break it in pieces" (Daniel 7:23b). It will become the ruling platform for the Antichrist.

> And it was granted to him to make war with the saints, and to overcome them – and authority was

> given him over every tribe, tongue, and nations. All who dwell on the earth will worship him, whose names have not been written in the Book of Life. (Revelation 13:7b-8a)

The Antichrist will control the world by using technology implanted within the human body. Those who refuse these implants will be unable to participate in the world economy.

> He causes all, both small and great, rich and poor, free and slave, to receive a mark in their right hand or on their foreheads, and that no one may buy or sell except one who has the mark or the name of the beast, or the number of his name. (Revelation 13:16-17)

True Christians will be the final enemy of this global government, for they will refuse to worship the Antichrist and reject the mark of the beast.

At the end of the age, both God's kingdom and the devil's kingdom will reach an apex. When they both come to fullness, the glory of God will shine out through God's people and shatter the darkness.

Arise, shine, for your light has come, and the glory of the Lord is risen upon you. For behold, the darkness shall cover the earth, and deep darkness the people, but the Lord will arise over you, and his glory will be seen upon you. The Gentiles shall come to your light, and kings to the brightness of your rising. (Isaiah 60:1-3)

Daniel reveals this final triumph.

And in the days of these kings the God of heaven will set up a kingdom which shall never be destroyed; and the kingdom shall not be left to other people; it shall break in pieces and consume all these kingdoms, and it shall stand forever. (Daniel 2:44)

I beheld, and the same horn [the Antichrist] made war with the saints, and prevailed against them; until the Ancient of days came, and judgment was given to the saints of the Most High; and the time came that the saints possessed the kingdom. (Daniel 7:21-22 KJV)

But the saints of the Most High shall take the kingdom, and possess the kingdom forever, even for ever and ever. (Daniel 7:18 KJV)

Then Jesus will return, and everyone will bow down to him as the supreme political leader. "Every knee should bow…and every tongue should confess that Jesus Christ is Lord" (Philippians 2:10-11a).

All other authority will be put under Christ's feet, and he will be King of kings and Lord of lords.

— *Kingdom Core* —

1. The kingdom of God will someday dominate the world politically.

2. In the meantime, God's people are called to submit to human governments.

3. God's government is a spiritual government, and it is only revealed by spiritual power - not by earthly weapons or elections.

4. Satan has spiritually dominated the world since the Fall. He reigns through the principalities and powers.

5. The devil is preparing the way for a global government. This government will be the political platform for the Antichrist.

6. As the church matures, she will fulfill her purpose to declare the eternal victory of Christ to the principalities and powers, toppling them from their spiritual places of power.

7. When the principalities and powers fall, the current governments of the world will pass away.

— *Prayer* —

Dear God, your plans for this world are amazing. Praise you for what you want to do in the earth. Thank you for the new heavens and the new earth that you are going to create. Open my eyes to understand the spiritual forces that are behind world events. I acknowledge that my real enemies are not people or governments, but evil spirits. Help me to see things as they really are and deliver me from deception. Help me to work with you in the building of your church, so that she can reveal the power of your word against every spiritual enemy. Deliver me from all fear and give me confidence in your victory. In Jesus' name I pray. Amen.

7.
Preparing for
Kingdom Fullness

THE KINGDOM OF GOD dominated the world in the beginning, and it's going to dominate the world in the end. When Jesus comes back, he's going to reign over everything, and his people will reign with him. Christians will be kings on the earth (Revelation 5:10). One Christian will rule over five cities, and another will rule over ten cities (Luke 19:16-19).

As we have seen, the kingdom of God is already here. Jesus is already the king of kings. The Bible says Christians are already kings (Revelation 1:6).

We are called to reign spiritually through Jesus Christ.

> For if by the one man's offense death reigned through the one, much more those who receive abundance of grace and of the gift of righteousness will reign in life through the one, Jesus Christ. (Romans 5:17)

We are "more than conquerors" (Romans 8:37) because Jesus has already won. He is *the* conqueror, and we benefit from his victory. That's why we are *more* than conquerors. It's time to accept our identity in Christ and believe in God's definition of who we are - a conquering nation filled with the Holy Spirit, called to reveal the kingdom of God.

We Need Vision

"Where there is no vision, the people perish" (Proverbs 29:18a).

As we approach the end of the age, God wants us to see the way ahead and be confident. We don't need to hunker down and wait to be rescued. God has a plan for his people, and he is expecting us to execute it.

Christians are not to be reactionary, waiting for bad things to happen before we formulate a plan. We are called to be visionaries who actively "hasten the day of God" (2 Peter 3:12) and speed up God's timeline. We need to act before the enemy does, making powerful decisions for God's kingdom through the leading of the Holy Spirit.

We need to anoint our eyes with eye-salve so we can see (Revelation 3:18). When we are able to see things around us according to the word of God, we will have vision. Then we will be able to move forward and fulfill God's plans.

One way to clarify our spiritual vision is to magnify God. To magnify something means to make it appear bigger than it would normally appear. A magnifying glass artificially enlarges small things, making tiny bugs appear larger than they really are. Don't magnify spiritual bugs like Satan. This will produce spiritual cataracts, clouding your vision and making you want to lie in bed with a sheet over your head until you can somehow escape.

We need to magnify God. He is much bigger than anything or anyone else in the world. No matter how much we magnify God, it will never be too much. The more we magnify God, the more accurately we see him. And the more accurately we see God, the clearer we will see everything else.

Our God is awesome. Let's revel in his presence and power. This will change the way we look at the future.

We must anticipate the revelation of Christ more than the arrival of the Antichrist. We must believe in the triumph of God more than the power of Satan. Jesus has destroyed death and given us eternal life! We need to know that God can preserve us in the midst of any difficulty and empower us to overcome any challenge. Let's adopt the mindset of spiritual conquerors instead of fearful slaves.

Fear is one of the devil's strongest tools. He uses it to create spiritual paralysis.

"Greater is he who is in you than he who is in the world" (1 John 4:4).

The Bible says that God will triumph, and that he will keep his faithful people safe. The Bible not only tells us about the dark reign of the Antichrist, but it also announces the impending victory of the kingdom of God. Let's believe in God and his power more than the devil and his power.

We know that global government is coming and persecution will rise. We know the Antichrist is on his way. Small chips will someday be implanted in people's hands or heads, without which they will be unable to buy or sell (Revelation 13:6-7). We can know these facts, but we don't need to be overwhelmed by them. God is greater than these enemies. He has already defeated them. The devil is not going to win, God is.

God has many ways to take care of us. When there was a famine, birds fed Elijah (1 Kings 17:6). When a crowd was hungry, Jesus miraculously multiplied bread and fish. Supernatural provision always follows those who are faithful to God. Jesus promises we will have food and clothing if we seek first his kingdom (Matthew 6:31-33).

Jesus is the Alpha and Omega. He is the beginning and the end. He tells us the end from the beginning. The end of the story is glory. We can be patient as we wait for the glorious culmination of history. God is weaving the eternal victory of his Son into the world, and he will keep on weaving this thread of victory until Jesus rules over everything. God is creating a glorious tapestry with the red thread of Jesus' blood woven throughout, and this beautiful masterpiece is about to be revealed to the eternal glory of God.

"We must through faith and patience inherit the promises" (Hebrews 6:12).

Necessity of Church

For God's people to fulfill their end-times purposes, they need to be part of Biblical fellowship. This is where true strength lies. God has people all over the world, and it's time for them to gather together according to the word of God. Where there are willing hearts and prayerful attitudes, God knows how to bring his people together. Let healthy, Biblical, radical churches arise!

Church is not defined by human tradition or organization. Church is defined by the word of God. We need to understand church as God wants church to be. Religious traditions have restrained the church for centuries, and it's time to throw off the shackles. God is calling his people to obey his word and gather together under his authority.

"Shake thyself from the dust; arise, and sit down, O Jerusalem. Loose thyself from the bands of thy neck, O captive daughter of Zion" (Isaiah 52:2).

Church is about to change drastically. Get ready to move from experiencing church as an occasional meeting to living in church as a community.

The early church lived together in house church communities, sharing everything. They met together daily and reached out to the world with the gospel (Acts 2:44). Jesus wants his body to be a community-based organization living not by their own strength, but by the power of God. The powerful church in early Acts is the model for the conquering church at the end of the age. Radical end-times saints will live together, share their possessions, and lay down their lives.

God's idea for church may be radical, but who cares? The Bible gives the only divine standard for church, and nothing else is going to work.

The early church didn't follow their own ideas; they followed the instructions of Jesus. Submission to Jesus is the key to all successful ministry. He is the head, and the church is the body. He is the king, and we are called to bow down. Where Christ is the head, his power flows into his body. The church's degree of submission to Jesus determines the extent of her ability to reveal the kingdom of God. Corporate obedience to Christ is why the early church changed the world.

Let's not be overwhelmed with the radical things God is calling us to do. Let's be overwhelmed instead by the awesome glory and infinite power of our majestic God.

It's not up to us. It's up to God. Through God, we can do all things. A new mindset will empower us to live as Jesus has called us to live. When we are willing to take Jesus at his word, obeying and believing, we will see his glory shine through us.

The church is to be an outpost on earth of the kingdom of God. It is to be a place where the kingdom is practiced, even if imperfectly. The great calling of the church is to be the beginning of the manifestation of the kingdom of God upon the earth.

The day of the individual Christian superstar is coming to an end. God has planned for his people to enter the Promised Land together. Strong individuals like Joshua and Caleb could not enter the Promised Land by themselves. They needed to enter with the entire nation. It's the same for us. No matter how spiritually strong we are, we are unable to enter the fullness of the kingdom of God by ourselves. We must connect with other believers in order to fulfill our individual callings.

As believers join together in Biblical ways, they will come into amazing synchrony with God and with each other. Corporate submission to Christ will unleash powerful manifestations of the Holy Spirit. Jesus will direct believers to do things which are interconnected with what other believers are doing, orchestrating powerful events which would be impossible to create otherwise. By listening to the Holy Spirit, the church will begin to move as a mighty, singular, worldwide body.

All across the world, thousands of seemingly small events will work together leading to a great confluence of events that will ultimately overwhelm the earth with the kingdom of God. We can hardly begin to fathom the far-reaching effects of Biblical Christian unity. Nations will be discipled when the body of Christ walks together under the headship of Jesus.

"You are the temple of the living God; as God hath said, I will dwell in them, and walk in them" (2 Corinthians 6:16a).

Not only are individual believers temples of the Holy Spirit (1 Corinthians 6:19), but the entire church is *the* worldwide temple of God. God is going to live and walk in the midst of his people. When this happens, the world will be transformed.

God has a plan for his church that can only be discovered in the pages of the New Testament. Church leaders and church functions must be defined by the New Testament in order to be effective. Believers must be willing to abandon the traditions of men and recover the word of God, in order that the true power of the church may be revealed upon the earth.

Ekklesia

In the original Greek New Testament, the word for church is *ekklesia*. This word originally referred to the group of people who governed a city-state in ancient Greece. An ekklesia comprised all the citizens of the city who met together to govern that city.

Now, the word *ekklesia* refers to the church. The church is the seat of God's government on the earth. It is the place of the earthly authority of the kingdom of God.

As we have seen, the church can only reveal the kingdom of God through the Holy Spirit. No other governmental methods are going to work. During the Middle Ages, state churches used force, money, diplomacy, taxation, bureaucracy, and other worldly methods to rule. These attempts to rule by the flesh all failed. They hindered rather than helped God's kingdom.

The basis of genuine church authority is the presence of Jesus. "Where two or three are gathered together in my name, I am there in the midst of them" (Matthew 18:20).

When God's people meet together in church, Jesus is there. Jesus is among his people in his ekklesia in a different way than he is with us as individual believers. Something special happens spiritually when God's people come together in unity.

The governing power of the ancient Greek ekklesia rested in the group, rather than the individual. It's the same for the church. Two people are the quorum for God's government, because two believers are all it takes for Jesus to be present. When a *quorum* is reached, enough members of a governing group are present so that group can make important decisions or take key actions. When Jesus is among his people, the government of God upon the earth can operate.

Pray Heaven Come to Earth

If we are going to see God's kingdom take over the world, we need to pray. Jesus said, "My house shall be called a house of prayer for all nations" (Mark 11:17b).

The church should be characterized by prayer more than almost anything else, for prayer is what unleashes God's power.

Jesus said, "If two of you shall agree on earth as touching anything that they shall ask, it shall be done" (Matthew 18:19).

When the quorum of God's government is reached, and two or more Christians agree with Christ and with each other and pray for God's will to be done, the governing power of God's kingdom can be revealed to impact the earth.

Prayer is powerful because it agrees with God. Prayer opens the door for God to move on the earth. Prayer is not about twisting God's arm, trying to get him to do something he doesn't want to do. Prayer is about saying "Yes" to his will, and opening the door for him to act.

Prayer opens the door for God's kingdom to come.

"The heaven, even the heavens, are the Lord's; but the earth He has given to the children of men" (Psalm 115:16).

In a sense, the earth belongs to humanity. God desires to work through people to fulfill his will upon the earth. God wants us to pray, so he can work with us to bring his kingdom into the earth.

Let's be audacious in prayer and agree with God to do what he already wants to do. Our prayers need to be as big as God is.

"Your kingdom come. Your will be done on earth as it is in heaven" (Matthew 6:10). That's a huge prayer.

In heaven, before God's throne, there is no sin. There is no sickness. There is no curse. There are no demons. There is no death! We are commanded to pray for the reality of heaven to become the reality upon the earth.

Do we believe this is possible?

Let's believe that God's kingdom *can* come, and that his will *can* be done.

Let's boldly pray: God, dominate the world! Demons be bound! Sicknesses be healed! Sinners be converted! Your will be done on earth, as it is in heaven!

Do we believe it is possible for God's kingdom to come all over the world? Can the earth become like heaven?

If we cannot believe that these things are possible, we should stop praying the Lord's prayer, because without faith, our prayers do not please God.

But let him ask in faith, with no doubting, for he who doubts is like a wave of the sea driven and tossed by the wind. For let not that man suppose that he will receive anything from the Lord; he is a double-minded man, unstable in all his ways. (James 1:6-8)

Let's pray for the mighty things that God wants us to pray for. Fervent prayers energize much. Pray for the kingdom of God to come completely and totally, everywhere, all over the world.

"You do not have because you do not ask" (James 4:2b).

Let's not limit God because of our lack of prayer. Ask for these awesome things in faith so we will see them happen.

Jesus said, "ask, and you shall receive, that your joy may be full" (John 16:24b).

Unanswered Prayer

Don't be discouraged by unanswered prayer. Sometimes prayers take a while to be answered. Two thousand years ago, Jesus prayed that all Christians would be in perfect unity (John 17:21). This prayer hasn't been answered yet, as the plethora of denominations today testifies. But it will be answered someday. If Jesus can wait for his prayers to be answered, so can we.

Jesus often encouraged us to keep praying and not give up.

"Men always ought to pray and not lose heart," he said (Luke 18:1b).

Unanswered prayers are part of the Christian experience. This is for one simple reason: it's not yet the end of the age. Think about it. If all our prayers were immediately answered, the age would be over. Why? We would pray for all sick people to be healed, all sin to be eliminated, all pain to disappear, and all graves to be emptied.

Imagine what the world would be like if every Christian prayer was answered! We wouldn't stop praying until there was no evil left anywhere on earth. God's presence would be everywhere! In other words, the fullness of the kingdom of God would arrive, and it would be the end of the age!

But it's not yet time for the end of the age. Therefore, all our prayers are not yet answered.

Let's keep praying until they are.

The Triumphant Gospel of the Kingdom

Before the end of the age, the gospel of the kingdom of God will be proclaimed throughout the world.

"This gospel of the kingdom shall be preached in all the world for a witness to all nations, and then the end shall come" (Matthew 24:14).

Jesus said *this* gospel of the kingdom would be preached all over the world - the same one that Jesus preached in the first century, accompanied by the same miracles and spiritual power. When it is, the end will come.

Imagine the ministry of Jesus happening everywhere. People going all over doing the works of Christ, in every town, every city, every nation, releasing the glory of God all over the world. When *this* gospel is preached all over the world, the glory of God is going to be released everywhere, saturating the earth.

Just as Jesus announced, "The kingdom of God has come!" in first-century Israel, so the church is going to announce the arrival of God's kingdom all over the earth. When the kingdom of God comes into the entire earth and Jesus reigns everywhere, the age will be over. Jesus will reign over the earth, and his people will reign with him.

Then one of the greatest prophecies of the Bible will be fulfilled: "The knowledge of the glory of the Lord is going to cover the earth as the waters cover the sea." This powerful prophecy is found both in Isaiah 11:9 and Habakkuk 2:14. This prophecy defines the future of the world. Through the church, the glory of God is going to saturate the earth.

When the kingdom of God reigns all over the world, the creation will be set free from corruption.

> For the creation was subjected to futility, not willingly, but because of Him who subjected it in hope; because the creation itself also will be delivered from the bondage of corruption into the glorious liberty of the children of God. (Romans 8:20-21)

Eden will be restored. Lions and other carnivores will eat grass like they did at the beginning. Mosquitoes will stop sucking blood. Snakes won't bite. Thorns and briars will disappear. Peace and joy will dominate the earth, and Christ will reign over everything.

> The wolf also shall dwell with the lamb, the leopard shall lie down with the young goat, the calf and the young lion and the fatling together; and a little child shall lead them. The cow and the bear shall graze;

their young ones shall lie down together; and the lion shall eat straw like the ox. The nursing child shall play by the cobra's hole, and the weaned child shall put his hand in the viper's den. They shall not hurt nor destroy in all My holy mountain, for the earth shall be full of the knowledge of the Lord as the waters cover the sea. (Isaiah 11:6-9)

Everything Adam lost will be fully restored.

The return of Jesus will be both a time of glory and of judgment. Everything and everyone in the world that is not according to God will be removed from the earth. All remnants of the kingdom of darkness will be taken away, and the spiritual fire of God will cleanse the universe from evil.

The creation will once again fulfill the great purpose for which it was made as glory and praise radiate back from the earth to God.

. . .

The Fearful Won't Enter

God had great plans for his people. He told them to go in and possess the best land in the world. They could just take over! There were terrible giants there, but so what? God was bigger and stronger, and he was going to bring them in. His angels would go before them and protect them from behind. All they had to do was obey, and the Promised Land would be theirs.

The Israelites couldn't believe it. "God wants us, a bunch of ex-slaves, to just take over such powerful nations? He wants us to conquer these giants and rule in their place? Impossible!"

Although Israel had just seen God crush the most powerful nation in the world (Egypt), they didn't believe he would do it again. Looking into the future, they couldn't see God's glory. All they could see was their own weakness.

They refused to believe God. They didn't want to go forward. They just wanted to escape - even run back to bondage. Their unbelief exalted the enemy. It denigrated God.

Because of their evil response, God consigned them to the wilderness for 40 years. Those 40 years didn't help them. They wandered around not until they were stronger and more capable, but until they were dead. Spiritual growth happens through obedience to God, not the passage of time.

"All these things happened unto them as types, and they are written for our admonition, upon whom the end of the ages has come" (1 Corinthians 10:11).

Move Forward

Jesus has already done everything necessary for God's kingdom to take over the world. He has defeated every enemy. His blood has taken away sin.

Now he's waiting for us.

It's time to wake up from unbelief and fear. We have to rise up and act. When we encounter the word of God, we have to do something about it, and that means taking what might seem to be a risk.

Stop wandering around aimlessly. It's time to submit to Jesus, become part of a radical church, and expect God's kingdom to break out into the world.

With God all things are possible. He's bigger than every enemy. We need to crawl up out of Saul's ditch and adopt the mindset of David when facing Goliath.

We don't need more armor. We need more God.
We don't need more time. We need more faith.
We don't need to escape. We need to win.
We need to trust in God, not in ourselves.

Launch out in boldness. Jesus says the violent seize the kingdom (Matt. 11:12).

God is watching. Heaven looks on in eager anticipation. Angels are poised, waiting for someone to act.

> For the Lord takes pleasure in His people;
> He will beautify the humble with salvation.
> Let the saints be joyful in glory;
> Let them sing aloud on their beds.
> Let the high praises of God be in their mouth,
> And a two-edged sword in their hand,
> To execute vengeance on the nations,
> And punishments on the peoples;
> To bind their kings with chains,
> And their nobles with fetters of iron;
> To execute on them the written judgment—
> This honor have all His saints.
> Praise the Lord!
> (Psalm 149:4-9)

Through the cross, it's all over. Every nation, every continent, all the dark reaches of the sea up until the highest mountains are going to be filled with God's kingdom. Nothing will be able to stop it.

This is a spiritual battle that Jesus has already won. It's time for us to believe.

- *Kingdom Core* -

1. The church is the seat of the government of God on the earth.

2. The word *ekklesia* defines the church as a governing body.

3. The quorum for God's government is two people, for when at least two people gather together in Jesus' name, he is among them.

4. In order for God's people to fulfill their end times purpose, they must recover the church as God intended.

5. The glory of God will radiate out through the church into the world, transforming the earth.

6. God calls us to pray for heaven to come into the earth. The reality of heaven is to become the reality of the earth. We must pray this prayer in faith, believing it will actually happen.

7. The end of the age will come when the gospel of the kingdom is proclaimed throughout the entire world, announcing the worldwide reign of God.

- Prayer -

Heavenly Father, praise you that your kingdom is going to take over the world. Help me magnify you. Anoint my eyes so that I can see the way forward. Forgive me for focusing too much on the enemy and being afraid. Let my future be defined by your word. Connect me with other believers who are willing to seek you above all else and become a part of the church as you intend. Father, I pray that all over the world your Spirit would awaken your people to your kingdom, and that your church would rise up and become the bride that is worthy of your Son. Speak to me, so that I may know what you want me to do. Help me obey you no matter what the cost. Fill me with your Spirit. Let your kingdom come! Let your will be done! In Jesus' name I pray. Amen.

Appendix:
The Political Consequences
of Free Will

> The authorities that exist have been established by
> God.
>
> *Romans 13:1b*

GOD ORDERS THE REIGN of the rulers of the
world - whether human or angelic, good or evil - because of two facts: God gave humanity free will, and he
allows human choices to have consequences.

1. God gave us free will. God did not put a fence around
the tree of the knowledge of good and evil and block

Adam's access to it. Instead, he put this tree in the garden to ensure that Adam had freedom to choose.

2. Human choices must have consequences in order to be meaningful. God did not put a fence around Satan after Adam's sin, blocking the devil from unleashing evil into the world, because Adam's choice had to have real consequences in the earth in order to be meaningful. Satan and his hordes legally won the right to reign on the earth through Adam's sin. God could remove fallen angels from power in the blink of an eye, but he doesn't do that because he respects human choices - even bad ones. This is how it can be said that God 'orders' the authority of Satan over the world. He gives meaning to human choice.

Without free will, we would be like puppets on a string. We could not be held accountable for our actions, and the concept of hell - eternal judgment for bad choices - would be absurd. It is ultimately God who preserves human freedom. Free will is important to God because it ensures that humans can love God, thank him, honor him, believe him, and be in a meaningful relationship with him.

God wants us to be close to him. For that, we must freely choose him. Where people are forced to love, love becomes hypocrisy. A chorus of robots programmed to praise is very different from a group of people who choose to praise. Praising from the lips is different from praising from the heart.

We choose God, and he chooses us. He has "chosen us in him before the foundation of the world" (Ephesians 1:4). Predestination is a doctrine that gives us security, knowing that our salvation is up to God and depends completely on him. But the reality of predestination doesn't negate the reality of free will. Both predestination and free will are true. Our limited brains find it impossible to reconcile these two doctrines. This theological conundrum is more complicated than quantum physics, which somehow proves that a single particle can be in two places at one time. How can that be?

The Bible teaches many mysteries. God is three persons, yet he is one God. Jesus is a man, yet he is also God. Jesus and the Father are one, but Jesus prayed to the Father and was forsaken by him on the cross. God chooses us, and we choose him. When faced with such mysteries in which revealed truth is clear on both sides of an issue, we need to believe both sides in order to have full, comforting, and accurate faith. Expanding our theology might hurt our heads, but it will heal our hearts. We don't need to understand everything about God because we cannot. He is infinite, and we are finite. He is God, and we are not.

Human choices affect world history because free will has meaningful results. Adam's choice lost the creation, and the human choice of Christ is the key to the manifested redemption of the creation. Throughout history, bad human choices have opened the gates of hell and released evil all over the world. Good human choices open the door for Christ to flood into the world with his light and kingdom. This is why Jesus commands us to seek for his kingdom, and not just wait for it to come. We must choose Christ for his work to advance in the earth. As we do, God will respect our choice, it will have meaningful consequences, and he will establish the rule of his kingdom over the world once again.

Kingdom Core

1. The main goal of the Christian life is to see God's kingdom come.

2. In the beginning, God's kingdom reigned over the earth.

3. Adam lost the power of the kingdom of God through sin, handing the world over to Satan.

4. Wherever the kingdom of God does not rule, Satan rules.

5. People naturally reject the kingdom of God because they are born in sin.

6. Jesus paid for the right for the kingdom of God to be completely restored to the world.

7. The kingdom of God is a spiritual kingdom, and it can only come by spiritual power.

8. Jesus and his apostles proved that it is possible for the kingdom of God to dominate the world.

9. Every manifestation of the kingdom of God upon the earth is based upon the blood of Jesus.

10. The restoration of the kingdom of God to the earth ultimately means restoring the conditions of Eden.

11. The kingdom of God comes into the earth whenever people obey God.

12. The kingdom of God is the only source of true peace, life, and joy in the world.

13. The will of God defines God's kingdom.

14. The will of God is often not happening in the world, and it won't happen completely until God's kingdom takes over everything.

15. The kingdom of God is inside God's people because the Holy Spirit is inside them.

16. God calls his people to externalize the internal kingdom – to release the Holy Spirit and transform the world.

17. The word of God is the seed of God's kingdom, containing the potential of his kingdom within it.

18. The kingdom of God will never stop growing.

19. The growth of the kingdom of God in the earth is a process of Christ's eternal riches entering history.

20. The kingdom of God faces Satanic opposition, because it is destined to overthrow the devil's reign.

21. The kingdom of God will ultimately defeat every enemy and rule over all.

22. Until its ultimate victory, the kingdom of God will not win every battle.

23. The kingdom of God and the kingdom of darkness will both culminate in the earth at the same time.

24. The emerging global government will try to destroy the true church.

25. God's kingdom cannot come through guns or elections; it can only come through spiritual power.

26. The church is the *ekklesia,* the seat of God's government upon the earth.

27. The church must recover her divine format in order to fulfill her divine purpose.

28. For the political power of God's kingdom to be fully revealed, the evil spiritual principalities and powers must be cast down.

29. When the church believes Jesus, submits to his word, and walks in his Spirit, God's kingdom will break out on the earth.

30. When the kingdom of God is declared all over the world with the full spiritual power of Jesus, the end of the age will come.

Contact

Visit

www.bethelcornerstone.org

More books by Peter John Brooks:

7 Foundations

Spiritual Technology

Where God is King

The Coming Glory

Goat Tags

Absurd Christianity